STAND UP TO LIFE!

STAND UP
TO LIFE!

DONALD E. WILDMON

Nashville o ABINGDON o *New York*

WILDMON, DONALD E. Stand up to life.
    1. Christian life—Methodist authors. I. Title.
BV4501.2.W5197   248'.48'76 74-30209

ISBN 0-687-39290-X

Scripture quotations noted RSV are from the Revised Standard
Version of the Bible, copyrighted 1946, 1952, and 1971 by the
Division of Christian Education, National Council of Churches,
and are used by permission.

Scripture quotation noted TEV is from the Today's English
Version of the New Testament. Copyright © American Bible
Society 1966.

Quotations noted TLB are from The Living Bible, copyright ©
1971 Tyndale House Publishers, Wheaton, Illinois. Used by
permission.

Excerpt on p. 28, copyright © 1974 by Ann Landers,
Publishers-Hall Syndicate, appeared in the Commercial Appeal
(Memphis, Tenn.). Used by permission.

Poetry on p. 19 is "Family Court" from Many Years Ago,
copyright 1931 by Ogden Nash. Copyright renewed 1959. Used
with permission of Little, Brown and Company and J. M. Dent &
Sons Ltd.

Manufactured by the Parthenon Press at
Nashville, Tennessee, United States of America

In Memory of
Hassel
1952-1973

Foreword

The Christian faith is practical. It is the guideline for the most practical way of living ever presented to mankind. More than anything else, the Christian faith helps us face the living of these days.

Why so many want to dwell so long on only the theological implications of the Christian faith is beyond me. To be certain, Christianity and theology are inseparable. But, for the Christian, so is Christianity and everyday living.

Wallace Hamilton once made the statement that Christ didn't come to get us into heaven, but he came to get heaven into us. That was one of the most profound statements I had ever encountered. It crystallized my growing opinion that salvation means more than going to heaven when one dies; it also gives a method of living in the here and now.

I am not to speculate on what heaven will be like. I do believe that it will be far more than we can ever hope for or imagine. But I feel that in the life and teachings of this Galilean, we can find the most practical and helpful approach to our daily living available.

I am no scholar. I profess no great knowledge or wisdom. You will not find written in the pages of this book any profound statements previously undiscovered. What I have to say deals more with the practical approach toward life based upon my understanding of the Christian faith.

Life is an uphill battle, all the way. Just about the time we think we have mastered life, something happens to disturb our contentment. So it appears to me that what modern man needs more than anything else is that which will allow him to remain in the battle and not be defeated. My Christian faith has helped me in this way. And if it has helped me, I am sure that faith in Christ can do the same for you.

What I have to say in this book comes from my experience in living and from my application of personal faith in Christ. I have written for one purpose—to share with those who read this. I hope that it will be of help to those who are, like myself, struggling to reach higher in a never-ending quest for life.

I firmly believe and know from my personal experience and the experiences of many people I have known that a person who follows the example of the life of Christ and his teachings and applies them in a practical way in daily life will enjoy life more.

It is Christ who gives me the power to stand up to life. And I know he can do the same for you.

CONTENTS

Stand Up to Life!

Some time ago I heard the rather humorous story of two men who were flying in an airplane for the first time. They were flying across the Atlantic on a trip that took approximately eight hours. Nearly halfway across, the men noticed that one of the engines of the plane had stopped working. Very shortly a voice came over the plane's communication system. "Ladies and gentlemen," the voice said, "this is the captain speaking. It seems that we have lost power in the number one engine. However, there is no reason for worry. We will only be about an hour late for our arrival."

A short time later the men noticed that another engine of the aircraft had stopped working. The voice was heard again. "Ladies and gentlemen, it seems that we have lost power in the number two engine. However, there is no reason to be concerned. This ship can fly on just two engines. We will, however, be about two hours late for our arrival."

It wasn't very long after that when the men looked out and saw the third engine had stopped functioning. Again the voice came over the system, by now sounding familiar to the two men flyers. "Ladies and gentlemen, I'm sorry to report that we have lost power in the number three engine. However, there is no need for worry. This ship was built to fly with just one engine working. We will only be about four hours late in arriving."

After the third engine had stopped working, one of the men leaned over to his friend and said in a very quiet, very serious, thoroughly disgusted voice, "You know, I'll bet if that number four engine goes out we never will get there!"

One of the greatest secrets in life is not to lose power in the number four engine. It is a necessity to keep flying life's route.

The death of Moses was a tragic event to the Israelites. He had led those people for nearly a half century. Then, at the time his people needed his experienced leadership most, he died. The loss of their leader nearly defeated their spirit and made them have second thoughts about entering the Promised Land. But then God gave reassurance of his presence to Joshua. "As I was with Moses," he said, "so I will be with you; I will not fail you or forsake you" (Josh. 1:5 RSV).

What God was telling Joshua and the Israelites was that they could still stand up to life, face their loss with courage, and carry on. The world had not ended as many of them thought. There was still power in the number four engine.

We all need to learn to stand up to life, to accept the hard blows life sends our way without letting them deal us a mortal blow. A person doesn't live long before he realizes one truth: Life is going to deal some hard blows.

Life is a series of ups and downs. It never runs on an even keel. Life isn't going to go our way all the time regardless of how hard we try to make it. We can't always have things the way we want them.

God doesn't expect us always to get everything we want, but he does expect us to do the best we can with what we do get. Even Jesus, who was God himself, didn't have everything go his way. Remember Gethsemane? And Calvary?

When life deals a hard blow you can withdraw into your dark corner and curse the world, or you can open up and let some sunshine in and reflect a little light out. The choice is yours.

Some good can even come from the hard knocks of life if you will learn from them. The person who refuses to learn from the blows of life passes up a great opportunity to become a stronger and better person. The person who does learn from them takes advantage of a golden opportunity.

Nothing is all wrong in life. There are times, you know, when many of us think that everything is all wrong. You have had those times and I have. But nothing is ever all wrong. Even a clock that has stopped working is right twice a day!

Life is worth living, but you have to work at it. It isn't automatically worth living. It takes effort on your part to make life that way. You can control your life, or you can let circumstances control it for you. You are the only person who can decide which route your life will follow.

Here's how Edmund Vance Cooke summed it up:

Did you tackle that trouble that came your way
With a resolute heart and cheerful?

Or hide your face from the light of day
  With a craven soul and fearful?
Oh, a trouble's a ton, or a trouble's an ounce,
  Or a trouble is what you make it.
And it isn't the fact that you're hurt that counts,
  But only how did you take it?

You are beaten to earth? Well, well, what's that?
  Come up with a smiling face.
It's nothing against you to fall down flat,
  But to lie there—that's disgrace.
The harder you're thrown, why the higher you bounce;
  Be proud of your blackened eye!
It isn't the fact that you're licked that counts;
  It's how did you fight—and why?

And though you be done to the death, what then?
  If you battled the best you could;
If you played your part in the world of men,
  Why, the Critic will call it good.
Death comes with a crawl, or comes with a pounce,
  And whether he's slow or spry,
It isn't the fact that you're dead that counts,
  But only, how did you die?

If we are to stand up to life, we must learn to make the best with what we have—not what we want, but what we have. There is a difference, you know.

I mentioned earlier the fears the Israelites had when Moses died. One assurance that Joshua and the Israelites had on their journey into the unknown was, "For remember, the Lord your God is with you wherever you go." Strength is available through which we can stand up to life—and it is ours for the asking. We only have to take advantage of it.

When everything seems to have gone wrong,

14

you can feel sorry for yourself and cry that life has given you a raw deal. Or you can take whatever life sends your way, stand up to it, and make the best of it. The choice is yours; just remember that you will never grow any stronger feeling sorry for yourself.

If you are to stand up to life, you need to convince yourself that: Absolutely nothing in life can defeat you unless you are willing to let it.

Many times, when faced with trying problems which life has put in our path, we feel that we are at the end of our rope. I have felt that way at times, and I know you have too. What should a person do when he gets to the end of his rope? Hang on! That's what the rope is there for.

A wit has put into poetry the tale of two frogs that had gotten to the end of their rope. One hung on, the other didn't. Here is the story of their plight.

Two gay young frogs from inland bogs,
Had spent the night in drinking.
As morning broke and they awoke,
While still their eyes were blinking,
A farmer's pail came to the swale,
And caught them quick as winking.

'Ere they could gather scattered senses,
Or breathe a prayer for past offenses,
That granger grand, that guiltless man,
Had dumped them in the milkman's can.
They quickly find their breath will stop
Unless they swim upon the top.

They swim for life, they kick and swim
Until their weary eyes grow dim.
Their muscles ache, their breath grows short,

And gasping, speaks one weary sport,
"Say, old dear, I've had enough of life, no more
I'll try it. Sweet milk is not my diet."

"Tut, tut, my lad," the other cries,
"A frog's not dead until he dies.
Let's keep on kicking, that's my plan.
We yet may see outside this can."
"No use, no use," faint heart replies,
Turns up his toes and gently dies.

Now the brave frog, undaunted still,
Kept kicking with a right good will,
Until with joy too great to utter
He found he'd churned a pound of butter.
And climbing upon this hunk of grease,
He floated to town with the greatest ease.

Now the moral of the story is this:
When in your Christian life you find
You're weary of the toilsome grind,
Don't get discouraged and go down
But struggle on, no murmur utter,
A few more kicks may bring the butter.

If you refuse to be bigger than the problems which life sends your way, those problems will defeat you. But if you can grow bigger than your problems, you will always have them on the run.

If someone were to ask me what my Christian faith does for me, I should have to reply that it gives me the strength to stand up to life. "I have the strength to face all conditions by the power that Christ gives me" (Phil. 4:13 TEV). That is a favorite verse of mine. Whatever else the Christian faith does, it gives a person power to stand up to life. I have experienced that truth in my own life many times, and I have seen it expressed in the lives of other people who would otherwise have been defeated.

As was said earlier—never lose power in the number four engine. Stand up to life. Be in control of yourself even if you cannot control your situation. And remember, "As I was with Moses, so I will be with you; I will not fail you or forsake you" (Josh. 1:5 RSV).

> I have hoped, I have planned, I have striven,
>   To the will I have added the deed;
> The best that was in me I've given,
>   I have prayed, but the gods would not heed.
>
> I have dared and reached only disaster,
>   I have battled and broken my lance;
> I am bruised by a pitiless master
>   That the weak and the timid call chance.
>
> I am old, I am bent, I am cheated
>   Of all that Youth urged me to win;
> But name me not with the defeated,
>   Tomorrow again, I begin.
>   —S.E. Kiser

Stand up to life!

How to Enjoy Living a Little More

Our Creator intended for us to enjoy living. Those who feel the Christian religion concerns itself only with life after death miss a major portion of the message of the Galilean. He was very much concerned about us in the here and now.

Using the common sense God has given us, and some guidelines Christ gave to approach life, we can set down some rules that will help us enjoy life if we will follow them—even enjoy life a little more than we perhaps do now.

The first rule is enjoy living a little more by laughing a little more. A good sense of humor has never hurt a single person, and it has made life blossom like a flower in the desert for multitudes. Concerning laughter, Sir Max Beerbohm once wrote, "Strange, when you come to think of it, that of all the countless folk who have lived before our time on this planet not one is known in history or in legend as having died of laughter."

Thomas Carlyle, the historian, believed in the medicine of laughter so much that he once stated, "No man who has once heartily and wholly laughed can be altogether irreclaimably bad." If you wish to enjoy living a little more, then laugh a little more.

Two men were fishing one Sunday morning when they heard the church bells ring, reminding the townspeople that it was time to come to church. One of the men, feeling guilty that he was fishing rather than being in church for worship, said to the other one, "You know, I guess we should have gone to church this morning." The other man, without ever giving it a second thought, replied, "Well, I couldn't have gone anyway. My wife is sick this morning."

And then there was the man who was having several distressing events happening to him at one time. He was telling a friend about his troubles. The friend, wanting to be of help to the man, told him, "Cheer up. Things could get worse." The man with all the problems said he took his friend's advice. He said he cheered up, and sure enough things got worse!

Another rule to follow which will be helpful is, enjoy your family a little more. Family life was intended by God to be an enjoyable experience. And it will be if we work at it, give it a little more of our time and effort. Children and grandchildren are to be enjoyed. So are parents and grandparents.

Here is some practical advice from the pen of Ogden Nash.

> One would be in less danger
> From the wiles of the stranger
> If one's own kin and kith
> Were more fun to be with.

In the world in which we live, the family unit is likely to break apart—at least mentally if not physically—if we don't make an overt effort to keep it together and fun to be a part of.

Business and a few of the other things which often seem so pressing can wait occasionally. The family unit only stays intact so long. So enjoy the family. Make it enjoyable to be a part of the family unit. Take the time and make the effort to enjoy the family a little more.

To enjoy life a little more, another rule to follow is to do what you enjoy a little more. Take some time away from your work for some recreation. The word "recreation" can be divided as re-creation. Doing the things you enjoy helps to re-create you.

We can become so absorbed with making a living that we can miss the joy of living. There is a speck of truth in the saying, "God made twice as much water as he did land. Therefore it is evident that he intended for man to fish twice as much as he worked!"

Now, we must remember to keep all things in proper perspective. We can overdo recreation as we can overdo anything else. So do the things you enjoy but don't overdo them. You will defeat your purpose.

The next rule is, if you want to enjoy living a little more, help others a little more. I have tried to make this a practice in my life, to be helpful to another individual. I know from experience that the times I have been able to help another person have made me enjoy life a little more.

I recall one Christmas when Lynda and I carried an underprivileged family a basket of food and candy. We just wanted to share with the family who were not as fortunate as we were in material goods. It certainly made our Christmas more enjoyable, and I think it did also for those we helped.

Say a kind word to another, a word of appreciation and encouragement. Help fill a need in another's life. The Carpenter gave us the secret when he said, "Treat other people as you want them to treat you." You will be surprised how much this will do to help make life a little more worth living.

Someone, we don't know who, said it in a poem:

I do not mind my "p's" and "q's," how careless
    I must be.
Nor do my actions always suit my neighbors
    to a "t."
I think perhaps my greatest fault that I now
    recall—
I make my "I's" a lot too large and all my "u's"
    too small.

Many of us, too often, have "I" trouble. It is the kind eyeglasses cannot correct. And this prevents us from enjoying life as much as we could and should.

To enjoy living a little more, here is another rule to follow—give a little more of your time and money to good causes. Time and money given to good causes can help make life more enjoyable for several people, yourself included. When you give your time and money to good causes, you are giving yourself. Your giving says you believe in those causes and in the good which they do.

One of the finest assets a person can have is a good attitude toward the money he makes. Our attitude toward money can make us enjoy using that money or it can make us miserable through the misuse of that money. Remember that your responsibility stretches beyond yourself. You are not an island. You did not acquire what you have without any help. You can use your money to help bring true happiness or cause you no end of misery.

If we want to enjoy living a little more, then another rule to follow is, worry a little less. Worry will not help you accomplish one thing you wish to accomplish, nor will worry help you avoid one thing you wish to avoid.

Robert Jones Burdette said, "There are two days in the week about which and upon which I never worry. Two carefree days, kept sacredly free from fear and apprehension. One of these days is Yesterday. . . . And the other . . . is Tomorrow." Of course, he missed the most crucial day, and that is Today. Speaking of worry, George Washington Lyon called it "the interest paid by those who borrow trouble."

It was the Carpenter himself who said, "And besides, what's the use of worrying?' What good does it do? Will it add a single day to your life? Of course not! And if worry can't even do little things like that, what's the use of worrying over bigger things?"

I'm not saying don't have valid concern. You must always have that. But learn to do the best you can, make the most of what you have, and leave those things you cannot help to God. Don't waste your health—mental or physical—on things over which you cannot have any control.

Do you wish to enjoy living a little more? Then worry a little less.

One final rule to follow if you wish to enjoy living a little more, love your Christ more. I realize that sounds religious, but we must remember that religion is a part of life. To ignore such a valid part of life is stupid. You see, every person worships something. What he worships determines his religion.

I know this fact to be true—the more you learn to love Christ, the more enjoyable your life will be. Life is a puzzle. It has many pieces. The secret toward an enjoyable life is fitting together the pieces. Loving Christ makes possible the fitting together of life's often baffling puzzle.

My experience has been that the Christian faith is the most practical element one can find to make life a little more enjoyable. It is like the sugar in the batter which makes the cake taste sweet. So if you want to enjoy living a little more, love your Christ a little more.

These simple suggestions which I have given to help us enjoy life a little more all have one thing in common—they are all a part of one's attitude. One doesn't need great riches to practice them, nor will great riches prevent one from practicing them. Whether or not you enjoy living a little more depends upon your attitude. Your attitude depends on what you choose to make it.

> With all its honey and gall,
>   With its cares and bitter crosses
> But a good world after all,
>   And a good God must have made it.
>   —Author Unknown

Take Time for the Important Things

Once the leader of the Scout pack of which my son was a member called me and asked if I would mind carrying a carful of Scouts to a ball game. I explained to him that I had a good bit of work to do on the day he needed me, but if he couldn't find anyone else to help out to let me know and I would make arrangements to carry some of the boys. He explained to me that he didn't think he would have much trouble getting someone to volunteer a car. "You are the first one I have called," he said, "and there are twenty-six boys in the pack." He expressed confidence that transportation could be secured from some of the parents of the boys but said if he needed me, he would call back.

Two days later the phone rang. It was the Scout leader. "Would you believe," he asked, "that I have called the parents of all twenty-six boys and nobody will be able to use his car?" "Yes," I told him, "I believe it. You see, I have had some dealings with human beings in this hurry-hurry society we live in." I told him that he probably had several who said they would really like to help but just couldn't at that time. He said that was correct.

The writer of Psalm 90, looking at the shortness of life, wrote, "Teach us to number our days and recognize how few they are; help us to spend them as we should" (90:12 TLB). That centuries-old prayer has never been more timely that it is today.

Life is short—very short. And, it seems, we are always busy—very busy. Had that Scout leader called me a few years earlier I, too, would have probably been too busy to carry a carful of boys to a ball game. But, you see, I had discovered a secret. I discovered that I was so busy that I was missing many important things in life and had decided to take some time for the important things. I now recommend that you do likewise.

Let me point out just a few important things which we too often don't have time for. Let us begin with education. God gave each of us a mind for the purpose of using it. I read recently that an authority who had researched the subject discovered that the average person uses only 10 percent of this mental capacity. Can you imagine that? Only 10 percent! No wonder we find ourselves in the situations we do sometimes.

I would imagine that many of us are like the schoolboy who came home after flunking a test in his history class. "Mom, guess what? I'm like Washington, Jefferson, and Lincoln." "How is that?" his mother asked. "I just went down in history," the young boy replied.

Others of us are like Uncle Noah. It seems that Noah, who had not had the privilege of formal education, was scribbling on a sheet of paper with his pencil. After scribbling for a few moments, he stopped and cried out to his wife. "Josie, come quick! I want to show you something. I just learned to write!" His wife picked up the paper and looked at it. Beaming with excitement, she asked Noah, "What does it say?" "I don't know," Noah replied, "I ain't learned to read yet."

Then many of us are like the student who was in the habit of saying "have went." His teacher soon tired of his incorrect English and required him to stay after school one day and write "have gone" three hundred times. When the student had finished with his appointed task, he discovered that the teacher wasn't in the room, so he left her a note. "Dear Teacher, I have finished my work. I am tired. I have went home."

I have a good friend a few years older than I who has told me many times that he often wished he had taken the time to go to college if only for two years. He said that it would have been of great help to him in his job.

Remember that formal schooling isn't the only kind of education. There is self-education. But that, too, takes time. Do you take the time to read good books, newspapers, and magazines? Do you make the time to take advantage of the educational opportunities afforded you? Take the time to develop the mind God gave you. Get an education and improve yourself. It is important that you do.

Another thing we need to take time for is to help in good causes. There are many worthwhile causes which need people to help make them work. We have already mentioned the Scouts. The United Fund needs your help. So does the PTA, the March of Dimes, and a host of other good causes.

Anyone who has ever been asked to secure other people to help with good causes knows how difficult it is to secure help. "I sure would like to help, but ..." And then they mention one of a hundred reasons why they can't.

It has been estimated that 20 percent of the people are responsible for 80 percent of the charitable work which is done. There once was an ad on radio and television which stated that for every boy in Scouting there was one who would like to be but couldn't because of a lack of adult leaders.

If you want to know the real reason more people don't become involved in good causes it is because they are lazy and selfish. They don't want to take the time. Thousands of people every day use many services provided by good causes without ever considering the fact that somebody had to take the time to make those services available, and others must take the time to keep them going.

Many of us don't take the time to enjoy our families. I was told once about a father who didn't attend a single baseball game his son played during the entire season. The father was too busy!

Lester Place once told this story in the *Moody Monthly*. "The greatest gift I ever received," said a young successful attorney, "was a gift I got one Christmas when my dad gave me a small box. Inside was a note saying: 'Son, this year I will give you 365 hours, an hour a day every day after dinner. It's yours. We'll talk about what you want to talk about, we'll go where you want to go, play what you want to play. It will be your hour.'

27

"My dad not only kept the promise of that gift," said the attorney, "but every year he renewed it—and it's the greatest gift I ever had in my life."

One of Ann Landers' readers once sent her this letter. "Will you please do a million mothers and mothers-in-law a favor and print this letter? Girls: Can you possibly arrange your busy lives so that you can find three hours a year for your mother and father and invite us over for a meal? It doesn't have to be anything fancy. Hot dogs and beans will do. You have had many suppers at our house and we are always happy to have you—and your children—but it would be awfully nice if you'd invite us to your place and let me be a guest for a change. Funny how kids seem to feel they are always welcome to pile in on their parents but they forget parents are people—and maybe Mom would like to be invited to dinner once in a while. They tell us all about the barbecues and dinners they give for 20 and 30 friends, but when it comes to Mom and Dad—oh, well." The letter was signed: "Our Phone Is Still Working."

A mother wanted the companionship and appreciation due her from her daughter. But the daughter didn't have time. She was too busy. The daughter, however, had time for nearly everything else.

Many of us are too busy. Take time for the family. It is important.

One other thing which we need to take time for seems important enough to mention. That is worship. For worship, regardless of what those who continually ignore it say, is important. And how would they know if it is important or not if they don't occasionally participate in it?

Richard Clarke Cabot once wrote, "Worship renews the spirit as sleep renews the body." We aren't all flesh and bones, you know. We have in our makeup a spirit, a soul. And that soul is the real person—the lasting person. Let me quote again from the wisdom of the psalmist. "I was glad when they said unto me, Let us go unto the house of the Lord" (122:1). If the body cannot live without sleep, neither can the soul live without worship.

I knew a man once who kept his business open ten hours a day, seven days a week. When asked about worship, he replied that he didn't have time for it. "I have to make a living," he said. So, in the process of making a living, he forgot to live. He had killed his real self, his soul, long before he died physically. You see, a person who doesn't take time out for worship always kills the growth of his soul, which is the real person.

Once I got a letter from a young man in prison. He wrote that since he had been in prison he had had time to read the Bible and had come to see that faith in God was important. He wanted me to visit his mother because, he said, she had been thinking about starting back to church. Chances are, in more cases than not, that if that parent had taken the time to take that young man to worship regularly while he was growing up, he would never have gone to prison. But she didn't take the time; other things were more important. Or at least they seemed more important at the time.

Worship is a habit—a good habit. It is a habit you must make yourself practice sometimes when you would like to stay away.

It was Henry Whitney Bellows who said, "I have never known a man, who habitually and on principle absented himself from the public worship of God, who did not sooner or later bring sorrow upon himself or his family." Emerson wrote, "And what greater calamity can fall upon a nation than the loss of worship."

Worship is important—vitally important. Take time for it.

Many of us are very busy people and there just doesn't seem to be enough time for everything we need to do. There may not be enough time. We may need to make time for some things, certainly for the important things.

"Seventy years are given us! And some may even live to be eighty. But even the best of these years soon disappear, and we are gone. Teach us to number our days and recognize how few they are; help us to spend them as we should."

Take time for the important things. They are worth taking time for. One day you will either be glad you did or wish you had.

When Someone You Love Dies

When David's son Absalom died, David's grief was so great that he wished he himself had died. "O my son Absalom, my son, my son Absalom. If only I could have died for you!" (II Sam. 18:33 TLB), David cried.

The hardest part of death is not the death of ourselves, but rather the death of someone we love. For more often than not it would be easier for us to die than for someone we love deeply to die.

I have some thoughts to share with you on this subject—the death of someone you love—and I hope they will prove helpful.

One thing we should do when someone we love dies is retain the precious memories we have. God has given us minds which have memory departments. We can retain memories of our departed loved ones. David never did forget his son Absalom. As long as he lived, David kept those cherished memories of the son he loved.

One day I was visiting in the home of a mother whose only son had been killed in Vietnam. The house was filled with pictures of him, and she told me about all his accomplishments. He had been an outstanding student and athlete. He had gone on to college and graduated from law school. He had only been married to his lovely wife a few months when he was killed. But the mother remembered him as her child, someone she loved. And those memories were precious and dear to her. That is the way it should be.

Mary, as any other mother, had precious memories of her Son. Shortly after the birth of Christ, after all the wonderful events that accompanied that birth, "Mary quietly treasured these things in her heart and often thought about them." Then, following the experience at the temple when the boy Jesus became separated from his parents, Luke passes over the hidden years of his adolescent life by saying simply, "And his mother stored all these things in her heart." Surely, at the crucifixion Mary must have remembered Jesus as her little boy growing up.

Mothers have no monopoly on precious memories because we fathers have them also. And so do brothers and sisters, and sons and daughters. Even friends have them.

Love is eternal, and it doesn't cease to exist simply because we are separated from the one we love—even if it that separation is caused by death.

In your memories, remember also that when someone we love dies they continue to live on in the influence they have on those who loved them. In one sense we are separated from them. But in another sense we can never be separated from them.

Then, too, when someone you love dies, ask God for extra strength in time of greater need. God knows you need extra strength when someone you love dies, and he is there to help.

Jesus once asked the question, "Which one of

you, if your child asks for bread, will give him a stone?" He went on to make the point that no parent would give his child stones if he asked for bread. And he pointed out that God loves us even more than we love our children and that he is much more willing and able to give us what we need.

Make good use of prayer. Prayer is a practical, powerful force through which we can gain strength. But don't expect, by prayer, to be able to relieve your heart of the pain it has. Don't even ask God to take away the pain. Ask him rather to help you bear the pain. Ask him for more strength.

You see, pain is a reminder that we possess love—and love is the finest quality we can possess. The pain is in our hearts because we love the person who died, and that love will never die because love is eternal. As long as we live there will be pain in our hearts because someone we love has died. We go on loving even after their death. When someone you love dies, remember the loving nature of God. Never forget that God suffers when we suffer, hurts when we hurt. Certainly the life and death of Jesus taught us that.

No man intentionally inflicts suffering on himself. Neither does God. No man, in a rational mind, would pick up his gun and shoot his son and then grieve because his son was dead. Neither would God bring about the tragic death of a child of his.

It is in God's plan that each of us die a physical death, but he does not dictate the method and time of death. When one dies in an accident, we all must accept the responsibility.

33

Some people feel that death, if it comes suddenly and unexpectedly, is a form of punishment by God. Remember that God is a just God, and no just God would destroy the innocent to punish the evil. No father, if he had a bad son and a good son, would punish the good son because of the evil deeds of the bad son.

We must, in dealing with the death of a loved one, remember that there is a difference in the Old Testament conception of God and the New Testament conception. In the Old Testament, God is often a God of wrath and vengeance. But in the New Testament God is a God of love and grace and mercy.

How is this apparent difference to be explained? Well, throughout history man has been trying to get a clear picture of what God is like. In the Old Testament, God was viewed through the Law, and then the Prophets, and also the Writings. But the real revelation of the nature of God never came through. So God chose to become man in the form of Jesus. And it was in Jesus that we get the complete revelation of the nature of God. No, it wasn't that God changed through those centuries. It was, rather, that man's conception of God changed because man saw God fully and completely and clearly in the person of Jesus Christ.

Death is God's law, not God's punishment. Always remember the difference.

We will never understand death completely, but we must learn to accept it as a part of life. Paul wrote to the Christians at Corinth, "We can see and understand only a little about God now, as if we were peering at his reflection in a poor mirror; but someday we are going to see him in his completeness, face to face. Now all that I know is hazy and blurred, but then I will see everything clearly, just as clearly as God sees into my heart right now" (I Cor. 13:12 TLB).

When someone we love dies, it should remind us to express our love to those who are living. We take life too casually sometimes, thinking we have forever to do some of the things we desire to do with those we love.

The older I get the more I realize that life is short, like a grain of sand on the seashore of eternity. Now is the time to show love, to enjoy friendship and companionship. Tomorrow the opportunity may be gone. Do the things you want to do, be the person you want to be with those you love now. Never take life for granted.

There is something else which will help when someone we love dies, and that is to remember that God has given us the promise of eternal life. Death isn't God's final answer, but life is.

As a youngster, I often attended church camp during the summer months. I remember that each evening, after we had all gone to bed, the bugle would sound taps. It was a signal that the day was over. But taps was always followed the next morning by the bugle sounding out reveille. It was the beginning of a new day. So it is with life. There comes a time when day is done and the sound of taps can be heard. But God's bugle will always blow reveille in the morning, and a great new life is begun.

35

Jesus said, "He who believes in me will never die." I believe that, believe it with all my heart. It is a promise given by God the Father, a promise we can trust.

As Christians, we can look forward to seeing again those we have loved who have died in Christ. Someone may ask what the next life will be like. Well, I can't give all the answers to that question, but I do believe that we will know one another in the next life. We will be able to talk and share together. And we will never again be separated from those we have loved.

Life beyond this life will be more wonderful than we can begin to imagine. We cannot begin to comprehend how wonderful that life will be, what God has planned for us after this life is over. Remember what Paul wrote to the Corinthian Christians, "No mere man has ever seen, heard or even imagined what wonderful things God has ready for those who love the Lord."

Two days after his beloved Charlotte died, Sir Walter Scott wrote in his diary, "Another day, and a bright one to the external world, again opens on us; the air soft, and the flowers smiling, and the leaves glittering. They cannot refresh her to whom mild weather was a natural enjoyment. Cerements of lead and wood already hold her; cold earth must have her soon. But it is not my Charlotte, it is not the bride of my youth, the mother of my children, that will be laid among the ruins of Cryburg, which we have so often visited in gaiety and pastime. No, no. She is sentient and conscious of my emotions somewhere—somehow; where we cannot tell—how we cannot tell; yet I would not this moment renounce the mysterious yet certain hope that I shall see her in a better world, for all that this world can give me."

When someone you love dies, remember that life is still worth living. Don't turn bitter when death comes to someone you love, no matter how it comes. But trust in God's goodness and love and in his divine wisdom, and remember that the separation which now exists is only temporary and that one day you will be together again, forever.

A Father's Prayer

Dear God, I need your help to be the kind of father I should be. Hear my prayer. Help me, Father, to be more interested in the things my children are interested in. Too often I find myself too deeply involved in my own thinking to pay much attention to what one of my children is saying. Remind me constantly that the things they are interested in are just as important as the things I'm interested in. Help me to be a better listener.

Then, Father, help me to set aside some time in my busy schedule for the children. It seems that I'm always tied up with something and then when I'm not I think I'm too tired to spend some time in their activities. Lord, help me keep my perspectives straight. Business can wait, but my children will only grow up once.

Help me not to forget that children need love and attention as well as food and clothing while growing up. Too many times I get so concerned about their material needs that I forget their emotional needs.

And Lord, I pray that my children will be able to see your love in me. If they can only see me living my faith then they will understand it even if I can't put it in the right words for them. Help me to keep important things important and secondary things secondary. You know that many times the temptation is to neglect the important things of life while concentrating on secondary matters.

Help me to teach kindness by being kind, forgiveness by forgiving, helpfulness by helping, and love by loving.

And, dear God, help me prepare my children for marriage by being a good husband to their mother. If I'm a good husband maybe it will help them when it comes time for them to take a life's partner.

Help me to look for my children's good points and to brag on them a little more. You know, Lord, that I won't close my eyes to their faults. As their father I must be able to see those. But Lord, help me to dwell on their positive points.

Another thing I will need your help in is having the power to say no to them when it should be said. We both know that many times a no is much better than a yes.

These children of mine are growing up, Lord. One day before long they will go out into the world on their own. They will choose an occupation. Help me to be man enough to rejoice in whatever they choose to do, and Christian enough to teach them that they can serve you in any occupation where they will work for the good of their fellowman.

Lord, I'm tempted to ask you to stop time, to keep my children little children always. But I know that life doesn't operate that way. So I will just ask you to help me enjoy my children while they are children. Then in my old age I will have beautiful memories of my children when they were small and be proud of them as adults.

Lord, I can't be a very good father without your help. So thanks for pitching in and giving me a helping hand.

Extra If Assembled

I was in a department store recently and noticed several new bikes on display. Since Timmy had asked for a new ten-speed, I decided to look at them closer. I noticed the price tag on one of the bikes. Underneath the price, in small print, was written $5 Extra If Assembled.

I started thinking about that—about how much that extra line applied to life. For life, you see, is like the bike—you have to pay extra to get it assembled. Life never comes assembled, even though we quite often wish it would. How easy it would be, we often think, if life came assembled in a neat package ready for instant use. But the truth of the matter is that it doesn't.

Each individual has to assemble his own life, put it together himself. And, like the bike in the store, we have to pay extra for the assembling. Now if the person who puts that bike together follows the directions which come with the package, that bike will provide years of service and withstand the bumps in the road over which it will have to be ridden.

And life is like that, also. Put your life together following the Manufacturer's guidelines and you will be able to meet the bumps in life's road without being damaged. Of course, if you pay no attention to either the instructions concerning assembling the bike or your life, you can expect trouble trying to make either operate correctly.

The Man of Galilee gave us the clue when it comes to putting our life together. "Seek first God's way," he said, "and the rest will fall in place." Despite many efforts, a better approach toward assembling life has not been found.

We are given life—but not as a finished product. We have to put some effort into it if it is ever to work right. You wouldn't dare take that box of unassembled bike parts, shake it good, and expect the bike to fall out of the box completely assembled and ready to use. Why, then, should one expect life to fall into place automatically? It is extremely more delicate and has far more pieces to be fitted together than the bike.

If your life seems to be hitting more and more bumps which are becoming rougher and rougher, it is probably because you have failed to follow the instructions in attempting to assemble it. You can, with your life as with the bike, reassemble it if it wasn't put together right to begin with.

And it is foolish to think that your life will automatically correct itself any more than the bike will. You have to expend an effort and follow instructions if you expect your life, or your bike, to be ready to meet the rough places in the road.

Personally, I want my bike and my life to be able to take the bumps. For that reason, I try to follow the instructions given by my Manufacturer as closely as I follow those of my bike's manufacturer. To me, it just makes good sense to do so.

I Saw God Today

I saw God today. Where did I see him, you ask? I saw him in the face of a small child whose smile and laughter reminded me of the happiness and joy that come from trusting a God who loves us.

I saw God today. Where did I see him, you ask? I saw him in the golden leaves of autumn which fall each year and blossom each spring. I heard him in the rustling of the grass and in the song of a robin redbreast.

I saw God today. Where did I see him, you ask? I saw him in the person of a teacher who loved his students. I saw him struggling to teach so that the student could have a better life. I saw him toil on in his labors, underpaid and often unappreciated.

I saw God today. Where did I see him, you ask? I saw him in the compassion of a doctor who was working with God to heal a patient. I saw him as with his skills and knowledge he helped relieve some of the suffering of a broken humanity.

I saw God today. Where did I see him, you ask? I saw him in the love of a father who was sweaty and tired from a hard day's work. I saw him work so that his family could have a house where they could make a home. I saw him work so that his children could get a good education. I saw him work so that the woman he loved could have a few of life's luxuries.

I saw God today. Where did I see him, you ask? I saw him in the person of a minister who wept with a family at the loss of a loved one, who joyed with a young couple at the birth of their first child, and who prayed for love which he could pass on to those with whom he came into contact.

I saw God today. Where did I see him, you ask? I saw him in a public official who was elected to office by the people. I saw him as he tried to do his best in a society which often accepts and fosters crookedness. I saw him as he struggled to make a decision, knowing that whatever decision he made would help some and hurt others, would be praised by some and condemned by others.

I saw God today. Where did I see him, you ask? I saw him in an ex-convict who was trying to make a new start in life. I saw him as his past life followed him everywhere he went. I saw him as he tried to start over and no one was interested in giving him the chance.

I saw God today. Where did I see him, you ask? I saw him in a person—any person, every person— who reached out his hand to help another. I saw him as people overcame the difference of race, creed, education, status, in order that they could help another.

I saw God today. Where did I see him, you ask? I saw him in the symbol of a cross. It reminded me of his great love for us. He loved us so much that he sent his only Son into our world to save us. His Son died for us even when we weren't worth dying for. I saw him on the cross, and I heard his prayer of forgiveness for those of us who put him there.

So you see, I saw God today. You say you have never seen him? You can my friend, if you will only look for him.

Believe in Yourself

Back during the first half of the eighteenth century, there was a young boy who aspired to be a writer. Because of his lack of formal education, the young boy wasn't sure of his ability. And his life had not been one that would foster self-confidence. His family had moved quite often, his father finally being jailed because of his inability to pay his debts. Because of the circumstances this young boy had been able to attend school for only four years.

To earn a living he got a job putting labels on bottles of blacking in a dilapidated warehouse. He found himself a place in which to sleep in a dismal attic, and he shared that room with others who couldn't afford anything better.

But this young boy was determined to write. He did write. Day after day. Finally he got enough courage to submit a manuscript to a publisher. He mailed that manuscript at night, when no one could see him because he was afraid someone might ridicule him. Soon he heard from the publisher. His manuscript was refused.

Time and time again this young boy submitted his writings. Again and again the same answer came back—rejected. No publisher or paper was interested in his writings. But the desire to write was burning in the young boy's heart and he refused to quit.

Finally, one of his stories was accepted. He didn't receive any money for the story, but the editor did give him some praise. It was such a happy moment for him that he walked the streets with tears of joy coming down his cheeks. Now someone else had shown some belief in him.

This bit of encouragement gave that young boy the impetus he needed to go on to greater things. And in a few years all of England was reading his writings. The young boy believed in himself, believed he was capable of reaching the dream he had for himself in his heart. For that reason, he would not quit.

Too often in life we quit too soon. Many times the victory is just around the corner if we would only keep trying.

It is of great importance that a person believe in himself. Selling ourselves short is no virtue. It is a vice. It hurts us. It keeps us from developing our God-given resources to become all that we can become—all that God wants us to become.

The dreams we have for ourselves—of what we can do and become—can come true. They can, that is, if we are willing to continue to work toward the fulfillment of those dreams with all the resources we have. But we must remember that the fulfillment of any dream requires dedication, sacrifice, and persistence on our part.

The young boy in London who refused to quit was Charles Dickens. His novels are still read to this day. He believed in himself.

Believe in yourself. God does.

47

Don't Become Defensive with Your Problems

Every one of us has problems. Now, we do not all have the same problems. But we do all have problems. No one goes sailing through life without hitting a high wave occasionally.

Too often, in our problems, we think other people turn their backs on us (and sometimes they do). But many times it isn't that others turn their backs on us. It is simply that we have a defensive attitude which causes us to expect others to reject us. In other words, we look for rejection on their part.

We need to remember, when we are in the midst of a problem, that not near as many people know about it as we may think. Human capability is such that we can't know everything about every person at all times. And that is good.

It doesn't help to face our problems by being "touchy" about them. I learned early in life that if you carried a chip on your shoulder someone would knock it off. So I try to carry my chip in my back pocket, hidden from the view of those who get their kicks from knocking other people. I will share my problems with my close friends whom I know will try to help and understand. But I see no need to broadcast them to everyone I meet.

Don't become defensive if you happen to have problems that other people are aware of. Your defensiveness will often cause you to look for faults. I was visiting in a home once where there were problems. Several people in the town knew of those problems. A young boy in that home had run afoul of the law, and it had brought embarrassment to the family.

As I was visiting, one of the parents remarked that they were in a certain place and a person whom they knew happened to be there. The parent of the young boy said that the other person didn't bother to speak. The parent thought, quite naturally, that the other person didn't speak because of the trouble the boy had had with the law and felt hurt because of it.

I then explained to the parent that the person who didn't speak probably didn't recognize the parent. That other person was probably concerned with the problems she had which the parent wasn't aware of. And the other person's problems were far more severe and serious. Yet very few people were even aware that that person who didn't speak even had any problem at all.

Don't follow your urge to become defensive when problems come your way. Don't wear your chip on your shoulder. Very few people will turn their backs on you because you have problems. And just remember that you aren't the only person in the world who has problems, we all do. Quite often another person might have problems which you know nothing about, problems far more serious than yours.

When you have problems which others are aware of, don't become defensive. Just treat people as you want them to treat you.

Two Basic Human Needs

Every human has two basic needs when it comes to the area of love. One need is to love, and the other is to be loved. These are two basic needs of the human personality.

Once while visiting in the hospital, I was stopped by an elderly lady in a wheelchair. She didn't know me and I didn't know her. But she wanted to talk with someone. She told me about herself. She had no family to visit her, but some people from her church visited with her quite often. Tears came to her eyes as she told me about their visits. They meant so much to her. This elderly lady needed a little attention, some affection, wanted to know someone cared for her, someone loved her.

We all have this need to be loved—to know that someone cares for us, to know that we are important to someone. It is a hunger in the human heart to be loved. It is a natural hunger, as natural as breathing.

Then, also, every person needs to give love. Robert Hugh Benson once said: "It is only the souls that do not love that go empty in this world." Give love, and love will be given you. Not always by all those you give love to and not always in the manner you desire, but by enough people to make life enjoyable.

I'm not a psychologist, but I have seen enough of

life to know that love must have an outlet. Unexpressed love can be extremely dangerous to the human personality. I have even seen unexpressed love turn to hatred. A home where love is given and received by all members of the family is a happy home. A home where one member fails to give or receive love is often a miserable experience.

I say again—love must have an outlet. I have seen couples who did not have any children love a pet as they would a child. Why? Because of the need to express love. Children are a part of God's plan to give parents an outlet to express love. So are our marriage partners. They are a part of God's practical plan to help us meet this need.

It is just as important to learn to accept love as it is to give love. However, you can accept love without giving, but you cannot give love without accepting. Therefore, the emphasis should be on giving.

Now, these two basic human needs must be met vertically as well as horizontally. We need to love God and accept God's love of us. The best way we can express our love for God is to love our fellowman. An unknown author has put it this way:

> I sought my soul—but my soul I could not see;
> I sought my God—but my God eluded me;
> I sought my brother—and found all three.

Each of us has two basic needs—to love and to be loved. Remember to give love and love will be given to you. Accept God's love and love him in return. If you will learn to do these things, life will be enjoyable and worth the effort it takes to live.

A Message on Faith

Faith. How much that word has shaped our world! How many lives have grown into personhood because of faith!

What is faith? A man answered that question two thousand years ago. He said that faith is the assurance that something we want will come to pass. He said that faith is to be certain of things which we can't even see.

Faith is when one dares to go farther than he can see, to be willing to trust without any evidence that he should trust.

How much faith does a person need? That question, also, has been answered. It was answered by a Galilean carpenter as he stood on the Mount of Olives and taught his disciples. He said if we had faith as small as a tiny mustard seed that it would be enough to work miracles.

What has faith done for people? It has put a song in their hearts. It has brought sight to their eyes. It has put movement into their muscles and joy into their lives. Faith has founded empires; it has established principles; it has changed the world. Those who have accomplished most for mankind have been people of faith.

Faith. Faith in whom? Faith in God first of all. For he is the Author of faith. And without faith in him all else loses its high purpose.

Faith in ourselves next. This, too, is of utmost importance. For it is doubtful that you can succeed if you don't believe you can. But if you have faith that you can, then you will find a way. And the whole world can't stop you.

And faith also in your fellowman. This faith will be shaken often and even broken at times. But you must never lose it. Because if faith in your fellowman dies then your hope for a better world dies also.

Above all remember that God has faith in you. That is the reason behind the cross. That is the purpose of the empty tomb. He has faith that you will choose the highest, the best, the purest.

Don't ever lose this wonderful thing we call faith. For life is dull and void and ugly without it. So keep faith—in God, in yourself, and in your fellowman.

Faith will pull you up when you are down. Faith will heal your wounds when you are hurt. Faith will help you extend a helping hand to a brother who has wronged you. And faith will heal the sickness in your heart.

Seek out faith. Find her. Pay whatever price is asked for her. And let her be your constant companion on the road of life. She will make you richer than all the money the world has.

Dealing with Conflict

In the Gospels there is a story of a man from Gadara who was at war—with himself. Inside him there was terrible conflict. We are told that so many different forces were striving to take control of him that, when asked what his name was, he answered "Legion." He was many persons, inside, and they were at war with one another.

How do you deal with conflict? The manner in which we answer that question has a tremendous bearing on how much we will enjoy living, as well as the condition of our emotional health.

The dictionary gives two definitions of the word "conflict." It defines the word as a noun and as a verb. As a noun, the word is defined thus: "clash between hostile or opposing elements or ideas." As a verb, the word is defined in this manner: "to show antagonism or irreconcilability." Perhaps we have too often looked upon the word as a verb, to show antagonism or irreconcilability, instead of as a noun—a clash between hostile or opposing elements or ideas.

Well, how does one deal with conflict? We can begin by recognizing that conflict, in itself, isn't necessarily bad, evil, or even wrong. Many people desire to avoid conflict because they have a belief that all conflict is wrong and should be avoided.

If you are a person who believes that all conflict is wrong, you need to remember that no constructive change in the history of mankind has ever been accomplished without some degree of conflict. This country would still be a pawn in the hands of England if our forefathers had believed all conflict was wrong. Freedom, individual or collective, can never be gained without some type of conflict. It is simply true that some goals are worth the conflict it takes to accomplish them.

Jesus was in constant conflict with the establishment, yet we don't consider Jesus an evil person—quite the opposite.

Conflict involves confrontation—but confrontation isn't always wrong. Consider the conflicts a small seed must go through to become a mighty oak. It is confronted with the conflicts imposed upon it by the elements of soil and weather. And it grows through those conflicts to become a great tree.

Conflict is inevitable when one strives toward something better. A runner practices to run better, and at the same time there are forces inside him seeking to hold him back. The result is conflict! A person strives to rid himself of prejudice, yet there are those who enjoy their prejudice. Conflict! The way things are at war with the way things should be. Conflict! Jesus was familiar with it.

Never teach your child to avoid conflict. To do so will impair his emotional stability. Teach him rather to face conflict in a positive and constructive manner.

In dealing with conflict, we should not—and

often cannot—continually avoid it. Too often our method of dealing with conflict has been to avoid it. I doubt that conflict can be permanently avoided short of death, and I'm not sure that some folks—especially those who can't stand hot places—can avoid it then.

We will deal with conflict much more successfully by learning to accept it as a normal part of growth.

Many times, to avoid conflict means to surrender that which we know is best. We could have avoided the terrible conflict of the second World War if we had surrendered without firing a shot. But would it have been the best thing to do? There are similar examples in our personal conflicts.

Conflict isn't always of our own making. Sometimes it is forced upon us and we cannot avoid it. There are those who would selfishly impose their way at the expense of others. To avoid conflict in such a situation would be to deny the very reality of God. Two ideas that stand opposed to each other must ultimately be faced. And when they are faced, conflict is created. But we must side with that which we believe to be best.

There are times when conflict cannot be avoided. A ship in the ocean is caught in a storm. It would be foolish for someone aboard that ship to tell the captain to avoid the resulting conflict. It is an impossibility. The ship is in the storm and must face the conflict whether it desires to do so or not. Likewise, a similar situation often arises in our personal lives.

We need to remember, also, that conflict does

not have to carry hostility with it. The definition says "clash between hostile or opposing elements or ideas." That means that hostility isn't necessary in conflict.

I recently saw a basketball game. There was a tremendous amount of conflict between the two teams. Yet I did not see any hostility at all. Why do we feel that, in our conflicts with other people, there must be hostility. Can we not differ in our thinking with others without becoming hostile toward them? If we can face conflict without hostility, it is one sign that we are mature.

Family life is much more enjoyable when individual members of the family learn to have opposing ideas—conflict—without hostility. And they are in a much better condition to deal with their differences constructively.

Why do people avoid conflict continually? Well, some do so because they don't have the intestinal fortitude to face conflict. They are weak and insecure individuals. They need, desperately, to learn that it is through meeting conflict, not continually avoiding it, that we learn to deal with it.

In dealing with conflict, we must remember that it can be constructive. Many times I have watched the diamond cutters in Israel place the gemstone against the grinding stone. When they do so there is conflict. But after the gemstone has faced the conflict it comes out a very beautiful diamond. In fact, the polished stone could never exist unless it first faced the conflict. So it is with life.

Consider the conflict an alcoholic or drug addict

goes through when he decides to change. But he can use that conflict for a constructive purpose if he is able to stay with it and come out victorious.

Did you ever stop to think that it is conflict inside a person which causes him to see his need for Christ? A person sees that something is wrong in his life, and he begins to set it right. He then is at war with himself—conflict! He is trying to make his better self, his real self, take command.

> Within my earthly temple there is a crowd;
> There's one of us that's humble, one that's proud,
> There's one that's broken-hearted for his sins,
> There's one that unrepentant sits and grins;
> There's one that loves his neighbor as himself,
> And one that cares for naught but fame and pelf.
> From much corroding care I should be free
> If I could determine which is me.
> —Edward Sanford Martin

Substitute the word "conflict" for the word "care" in the next to the last line and you will discover the need for the real you to take command. For the individual, perhaps the greatest conflict, certainly the one which should be solved first, is the internal one. A person never needs to be at war with himself.

Did you ever see the television program "To Tell the Truth"? On that program they ask, "Will the real (contestant) please stand up?" We don't need to be at war with ourselves. This is what the Galilean helps us to do—end the conflict with ourselves. He helps the real us stand up.

One of the fruits of the Spirit is peace, inner

peace. The man from Gadara was many persons. But when his life came into contact with the Galilean he became one person. The real person stood up. The conflict inside him ended. He found inner peace.

Is there such a thing as Christian conflict? My answer to that question is yes, if through that conflict we can help another or become better persons ourselves.

Don't fear conflict, nor continually avoid it, if through that conflict you can help another or become a better, stronger person yourself.

When it is necessary to face conflict, do so with certain strengths. Face it with control, composure, character, and commitment. Maintain control over yourself, keep your composure, use the character which is highest and best, and stay committed to the best there is in you. If you do so, you can deal successfully with conflict.

Getting What We Want

In life a person should be sure that what he is working toward is what he wants. Too many times a person spends his life working toward a goal, and then when he reaches the goal discovers that he really didn't want what he got.

Marjorie Merriweather Post, who was sometimes referred to as "Grand Dame" Post, spent much of her eighty-six years climbing society's ladder. She became one of the nation's leading society queens. However, toward the end of her life, she expressed regrets at having spent so much time at the top.

At one of the last parties she held, while surrounded by gushing women, she leaned over to a friend and confided, "To think I worked fifty years just to have these bitches bow and scrape to me."

One of the cruel tricks which life plays on us is to give us that which we ask for. And many times we discover that the more we get of what we want the less we want what we get.

In ancient Greek mythology there was a story of one Midas. Midas had done the gods a favor, and his reward was that any one wish he had would be fulfilled. Midas wished that everything he touched would turn to gold. His wish was fulfilled. He nearly starved to death before he got it changed!

Some time ago there was a special program on television about several bright young executives who were apparently on their way up in the business world. The report told how one by one they had turned their backs on the climb to the top and accepted jobs paying much less. The more they got of what they wanted, the less they wanted what they got.

A person should be sure, before he sets out working toward something, that what he is working toward is what he wants. For the chances are pretty good that he will get what he wants.

To me the most terrible frustration life could give would be to spend your whole life in pursuit of something, and then when you finally get it, discover that it wasn't worth pursuing at all.

I remember reading a story about a restless young boy who wanted to be free—away from the restraints and restrictions of his father. So, he left home one day in a sullen mood and headed toward a place where he could do as he pleased. But the story went on to point out that the more he did of what he wanted, the less he wanted to do what he did. And then one day he came back home to do something worthwhile—be the son of his father.

Make sure that what you are working for in life is worth working for. Give it close examination before you decide to invest your life pursuing it. Weigh it on the scales of life. Compare it with the virtues of love and service. Don't waste your life in pursuit of that which you do not want.

I know of few disappointments in life that would be more crushing than working for something and getting it, only to discover it wasn't really what you wanted at all.

Dream Great Dreams

No one should be afraid to dream. Indeed, every person should have some dreams of his own. Dreams help make life more enjoyable.

Someone has stated that we should climb until our dreams come true. Of course, that is presupposing that we have dreams to climb toward. Most of us do. Those who don't, should.

Dreams will be as different as the people who have them. And why shouldn't they be? After all, they are personal. We do our own dreaming, no one else can ever do it for us.

I'm a dreamer myself. I always have been. I hope I always will be. Some of my dreams seem unrealistic and impossible. But no matter how far removed they may seem, they are still possible as long as I continue to pursue them. Even if I never accomplish my dreams, they have been of value to me. For they have given me a goal to reach for, and a desire to press toward that goal. They have helped me keep trying when defeat seemed ever so close and when I wanted to quit.

In one way, dreams aren't expensive. They don't cost any money. Even the poorest person in the world can have all the dreams he desires. But in another way they are expensive. For we have to work and sacrifice to make our dreams come true. There just aren't many Prince Charmings around who will pop out of nowhere to make our dreams come true without any effort on our part.

I believe this ability to dream which we humans have is one of God's great gifts to us. It has caused us to press on, to advance, to try to climb higher than we are. And in this respect we are indebted to God. Therefore, our dreams should be toward some goal that would make life richer for others as well as ourselves.

One thing I know for certain, God wants us to be somebody, to do something worthwhile. He never intended for a single one of us to be a nobody—to waste life.

I hope you are a dreamer. And I want you to remember that your dreams don't have to include fame and fortune to be worthwhile. A woman who dreams of being the best possible mother has a very noble dream. A person who dreams of being kind and loving to other people has a dream worthy of pursuit.

The world, and those of us in it, are greatly indebted to the dreamers. Our lives would be much the poorer without them. Their contributions to mankind can never be measured.

Get captured by a great and worthy dream. Then pursue it. Pursue it with your whole self. Never stop pursuing it. Great and worthy dreams can come true. They have come true. And remember that everything began as a dream. As Carl Sandburg said, "Nothing happens unless first a dream."

Dreams can come true. But even if they don't, life will be more rewarding for the person who dreams.

On Camels and Gnats

I read a story not long ago about a lady by the name of Jennie Grossinger. The article said that she was the founder and owner of Grossinger's, a 1200-acre, world-famous resort in the Catskills. The article told of a special problem she had in the 1940s when the big-name entertainment she hired was beginning to draw a large non-Jewish trade. The resort had never presented entertainment on Friday night, the eve of the Jewish Sabbath.

Mrs. Grossinger consulted a Talmudic scholar who told her that Sabbath-eve entertainment would be permissible as long as the resort was not owned by a member of the Jewish faith at that time.

So, the article stated, every Friday she would solemnly present the deed to Grossinger's—worth about twenty million dollars—to Hans Behrens, a longtime, non-Jewish employee. Behrens would then buy it for one dollar and become the "owner" until Saturday night. On Saturday night Mrs. Grossinger would buy the place back.

Reading that story reminded me of Herod the Great, the ruler in Palestine at the time of the birth of Christ. Herod was not a Jew, but for political convenience he had adopted the Jewish religion. He was trying to win the favor of the Jews he ruled.

Herod was a stickler for Jewish law. He consistently refused to eat any pork because it was against

Jewish law. But Herod had no qualms about killing his wife, his brother-in-law, and three of his sons. His actions led his Caesar, Augustus, to comment that he would rather be Herod's pig than Herod's son!

It is sad when one's religion becomes so legalistic that it misses the spirit. The Christian religion, as taught by the Founder, is not one concerned with a legalistic approach, but a spiritual one. He even told a parable one day, the last half of which we have conveniently forgotten. You recall the part of the parable dealing with the prodigal son. But do you remember the last part of the parable—the part concerning the elder son.

It was the elder son who stayed home and did all the chores. He never wasted his father's money. He did what he was supposed to do. He did it when he was supposed to do it. But he did it all in the wrong spirit. He gained little joy from it, missed completely what his father had tried to teach him.

I guess there is a way to get around every rule in the Christian religion, if a person is smart enough to do so. But there is no way to get around the spirit of the religion.

You can deed your property over one day a week if you wish. Or you can avoid eating pork. But my question is, why even bother with religion at all if this is your approach? If your religion is a burden instead of a joy, then you have missed the point of it.

In any religion, you may be able to stay legally clean while getting spiritually dirty. Even in this day it is possible to swallow a camel and choke on a gnat.

Important Rules for Living

Let us suppose there were two men who were setting out on a long journey through unfamiliar territory. Before they began their journey, each of the men was given a road map. By using this map they could easily find the way to their destination.

One of the men took his road map and used it, studying and following its rules and directions. The other man, thinking that he knew all that needed to be known and finding that a road map was unnecessary and unpleasant to follow—and even belittling to his pride—threw his away. He didn't see any need for a map and completely ignored it.

Now you know as well as I do the end result of each man's trip. The one who followed the directions of the road map would arrive at his destination as quickly and easily as possible. The other man would get lost and arrive at his destination only after a long and trying ordeal—if he ever arrived at all.

Life is a journey into the unknown. None of us has ever traveled the road of life before. It is a completely new territory. Therefore, the rational and sensible man will be aware of the helps available toward a more pleasant and enjoyable trip. The irrational and insensible man will ignore those helps.

God has made available to each of us information for use on this unknown journey. This information I will call "Important Rules for Living." Follow these rules and life will be much easier and more enjoyable. Ignore them and trouble will be coming your way. Let me share some of these important rules for living with you.

One important rule for living is this—keep life as simple as possible. Life is complicated enough without any effort on our part to make it more so. You will enjoy life more if you keep it less complicated. And one thing is certain—God intended that you enjoy life as much as possible.

Another important rule for living—learn to like your work. It can be your friend. It is work which gives us a chance to be creative, to make a contribution to the world in which we live. It is work which allows us to earn a living, to put food on our tables, to clothe our children, and to provide a shelter over our heads. Work can be a real drag or a real challenge. It will be what we make it.

There is something wrong with either you or your job if you get up hating to go to work. Chances are the wrong isn't in your job but in your attitude. And if your job isn't all that you want it to be, that isn't too surprising. Very few of us ever get the ideal job.

Many people want a big job because they think a big job will make them a big person. They are wrong about that. A big job never makes a big person. But a big person can make nearly any job an important one. So learn to like your work. It can be your friend.

Another important rule for living is to have a good hobby. A hobby helps you relax, helps relieve some of the pressure you face in your work. Many times in life a person will find himself up against a brick wall. It is a wise person who, instead of beating his head against the wall in despair, can turn to a hobby and find some relaxation while giving himself time to figure out a way to get over, under, or through that wall.

Have you heard about the man whose hobby was hunting? His wife was continually wanting him to take her on one of his hunting trips. She pestered him until he finally gave in and agreed to take her deer hunting. He placed her in his favorite stand and told her to wait until a deer appeared and then shoot it. He went on a little distance from her and got in another stand. Everything was very quiet for about three hours, and then he heard five shots which his wife had fired.

Deciding that he had better check on her, he got down from his stand and went to where he had left her. As he walked he saw another hunter in front of his wife's stand. The two were talking. The husband caught the final part of the conversation.

"Yes, ma'am, that is your deer," the hunter said as he stood with his arms up in the air. "I shot that deer," the woman shouted out. "Yes, ma'am, you sure did shoot that deer," the man replied as he continued to hold his arms in the air. "I'm going to take that deer home with me because it belongs to me," the woman shouted back. The man replied, "Yes, ma'am, you can have the deer to take home with you. You shot it. You killed it. It is your deer." There was a short pause, and then the man spoke again. "Before you take the deer home, could I ask just one little favor of you?" "What do you want?" the woman asked. "Would you mind if I took my saddle off the deer before you carried it home?"

Another important rule for living is to love people. When you fall in love with people, many of them will fall in love with you. And they will make life much more enjoyable for you. You will be surprised to learn how much better people become when you begin to love them. We want other people to love us. Then why not treat them with the same courtesy and kindness which we desire? Love them; it is a simple application of what is commonly known as the Golden Rule.

The most-loved people I have known have been those who loved the most. They weren't the richest or smartest, they didn't even have the best physical health. But they had a genuine love of people, and that made life an enjoyable experience for them. You will find that when you fall in love with people you will also fall in love with life.

Learn to love—it is an important rule for living.

Think and say cheerful and pleasant things— another important rule for living. What a man thinks determines his attitude. I have discovered that people enjoy the company of those who have cheerful, pleasant things to say. And I know, also, that none of us cares to be around those who are continually complaining.

Life is so much easier and more enjoyable when you think and say cheerful, pleasant things. Get rid of all your bitterness. Forgive those who have wronged you. Don't hold grudges against others.

Quite often Jesus would ask someone, "What do you think?" He knew that it was vitally important what a man thought.

Still another important rule for living is to never let a loss defeat you. You will lose a few battles in life. You can expect that. But you must never lose the war. Even Jesus lost a few battles. But he didn't lose the war.

Perhaps you have lost some battles lately, some really serious battles. But you mustn't surrender to the doubt and despair. The war isn't over, and you still have everything necessary inside you with which to win. Today is a new day. This is another chance to start over. Never let a loss defeat you.

Here is another important rule for living—meet your problems with decisions. Don't think that the choices we desire will always be open to us. Most of our decisions will be based not on what we want to do, but on what we can do. So take the best of the choices available and act on it.

Remember, also, that none of us will always make the right decision. There will be times when we will decide wrongly and will have to reverse our decision. But make a decision and act on it. Even a wrong decision is often better than indecision.

Have a goal toward which you are working. This is another important rule for living. Know what it is you wish to accomplish in life and then go after it. Always keep moving that goal higher and higher as you begin to approach it. Without a goal you only exist. With a goal you can live.

The other important rule for living which I have

found is to have a vital, living faith in Jesus Christ. Many questions in life will baffle you. You will never find answers to some of those baffling questions. But you can find the answer in the person of Christ.

"Faith is not belief without proof," said Elton Trueblood, "but trust without reservations." And it was J. G. Holland who wrote, "Faith draws the poison from every grief, takes the sting from every loss, and quenches the fire of every pain; and only faith can do it." So have a vital, living faith in Christ.

These, then, are some important rules for living: keep life as simple as possible, learn to like your work, have a good hobby, love people, think and say cheerful and pleasant things, never let a loss defeat you, meet your problems with decisions, always have a goal toward which you are working, and have a vital, living faith in Christ. Remember them and practice them.

The Christian Mechanic

You know, in all my life I have never read an article about how pleasing it was to God when a person decided to become a mechanic. I have read articles and heard sermons which have lifted up the ministry and medicine and teaching. But I have never seen one word in print about the sacredness of the mechanic.

That is a shame. It says something about our society. Somehow we think that one job is holier than another. And that isn't true. Because the job is no holier than the man who performs it.

If I understand the teachings of the Carpenter on this subject, then each and every task he gives us to do is equally important. Therefore a Christian mechanic is just as important in God's work as a Christian minister. Now I know it is the minister who preaches the sermons and leads the congregation. Maybe that's why we feel his job is more important—he is always seen and heard.

But, as I understand the teachings of the Galilean, any occupation can be a holy trust from God as long as the person who fulfills that occupation sees himself as God's servant.

A lot of folks, when they think of the mechanic, think that the profession is full of crooks and cheats. Well, the mechanics aren't any different from any other group. That means that often there is a rotten apple in the barrel, just as there is in the ministry or any other profession. But, remember that just because some of them happen to be crooks doesn't mean all of them are. By and large the vast majority of mechanics are honest people trying to make an honest living.

Any occupation can be a holy occupation—if the person is. This means that we all are of equal importance in the eyes of the Creator—minister, mechanic, plumber, housewife, or whatever. We just have different duties to perform.

Did you ever stop to think how dependent our society is on the mechanic? Where do you go when your car stops running? Who do you turn to if an appliance is out of whack? The mechanic is a repairman. He has this role in common with the minister, the dentist, the doctor, and a host of other people.

I think God rejoices when one of his children decides to become a mechanic or when a mechanic decides to become one of his children. For he needs his children involved in all occupations.

Yes, sir, God does use ministers. But he uses mechanics equally as well. You see, God isn't concerned as much with the kind of work we do as he is with the kind of persons we are. And that means the Christian mechanic is just as important as the Christian minister.

Thanks, Mama

Thanks, Mama.

That's about the best way I know to say it. For all the things you gave me and did for me in my formative years. I'm a grown man now, and I can look back at my life at home with more objectivity than when I was growing up.

Thanks, Mama, for taking me to church. I can remember when we lived quite a long way from church. But come Sunday we went. I can remember that my clothes weren't quite as fine as the other kids's clothes, but that didn't stop me from learning about the love of God. And there was that stage I went through when I rebelled against attending church. I remember the day I went to Sunday school and then skipped church. I remember getting home and the lecture you gave me. I went the next time. I may not have wanted to, but I did. And I'm richer because of it, because you cared enough to discipline me.

Thanks, also, for standing beside me during trying times. I recall the time in high school when the principal and I had a misunderstanding. I thought I was doing what was right and was standing on a principle. And you stood beside me. If there was ever a doubt in your mind as to whether or not I was doing what was right, it never showed. I believed you believed in me. And I needed, desperately needed, that belief at that time.

Thanks, too, Mama, for working so I could have an education. I still remember that night I came home from my first few days in college and said I was quitting. You talked me into finishing that semester and several more. And during those days, little did I realize the sacrifice you were making. I look back now and realize that we were poor folks, and it took all the money you and Daddy could make to give us children a chance at an education. It never entered into my mind at that time that we weren't as well off as other people. I guess I just took it for granted that we were. I knew you hardly ever bought a new dress or went to the hairdresser. But at that time I didn't know women were supposed to do things like that.

Thanks, also, Mama, for instilling high morals in me. I recall the day I caught my shirt in the screen door and let out a little four-letter word. I was really shocked to see you standing there. And the silent disappointment that was on your face spoke more than harsh words of condemnation could have ever said.

Looking back now I can see we didn't have much of the world's goods. We weren't accepted by many folks because we were kinda poor. But I learned what honesty was and fairness and love. And I want you to know that I wouldn't trade what you gave me for all the "riches" of those folks who thought we weren't "good enough" to associate with them. I guess we may be good enough now, and if we are it is because our love reaches just a little farther than theirs.

In closing, let me add there are many things I could say thanks for. But allow me to sum them all up by simply saying thanks for your love. It was that that made you the type mother you are.

Thanks, Mama.

A Father's Influence

Dear Daddy,

Once every year they have a special day for fellows like you. They call it Father's Day. And on that day we children are supposed to honor you.

Somehow that just doesn't seem right. Oh, not that you shouldn't be honored. You deserve that. But that we should have a special day to do it. Somehow I have an idea that every day is, for fathers like you, a Father's Day. For every day, folks like myself go through life, make decisions, pass judgments, and in general live out our lives on principles that our fathers taught us.

Often I think about what would have happened to me if I ever started looking to the bottle to solve some of my problems. I know many people who have. They used to say that one person in every sixteen who drinks becomes an alcoholic. The figure is probably a little higher than that nowadays. But I don't have to worry about becoming an alcoholic for the simple reason that you taught me not to drink. I remember very clearly, when I was but a youngster, asking you about drinking. You told me that you never did. That solved the thing for me then and there. If you didn't drink, then I knew I shouldn't either.

I sincerely try to treat people fairly and honestly—to treat them as I would like to be treated. In other words, I try to apply the Golden Rule to my life. Where did I learn this? Not so much from my Sunday school teacher or preacher as from you. Oh, I know you never sat me down and made me memorize it. But I learned it as I saw you practice it in your daily life. And memorizing it wouldn't have helped much unless I saw you practicing it.

You never gave us children much money for the simple reason that you didn't have much. You would have given us your last penny if we had needed it. I know that. But you gave us something worth many times over the value of money. You gave us a good name. I have always been proud to carry a part of your name. I do so with head held high. Seems that I remember somewhere in the Good Book it says a good name is to be chosen rather than great riches. I believe that.

As I grow older in years I grow continually more thankful for your influence on me. I cannot knowingly cheat a man or tell a lie or do any other thing which is wrong for the simple reason that as a growing boy you taught me an honest, better way of living.

Most folks measure success today by how high you rise or how much money you make or how powerful you are. Those criteria are false. And those persons who measure success by them are fools. The successful people are people like you. They are people who give their children real riches, spiritual riches.

I have many ambitions in this life, Daddy. You know that. But ranking high on the list is this one: To be as good a father to my children as you were to yours. If I can do it, I, too, can be successful.

Thanks for giving me a good start.

The First Stone

I went into a business to see a buddy of mine recently. While I was talking with him I noticed a rock about the size of my fist on a counter. On the rock was written Number One. I was curious as to what those words meant. I tried to figure it out, but finally gave up and asked my friend the meaning.

He told me it was the first stone. I was still puzzled by it all and was racking my brain to tie together the significance. Then he told me the story of the woman caught in the act of adultery who was brought to Jesus. The law required that the woman be stoned to death. Stoning was the Jewish method of execution. Those in the crowd asked Jesus what to do with the woman. Their desire was to stone her. Jesus stooped down and wrote in the dirt. Then he looked up and answered them. "Let the person among you who is without sin throw the first stone." One by one they all walked away. Then Jesus forgave the woman and told her not to sin again.

The first stone. It might not be a bad idea if we all had a first stone lying around close by to remind us of our need to forgive. It is awfully easy sometimes to see the other person's sin while ignoring our own.

Too often we can get so pious and perfect that it causes us to look down on another in scorn and shame. When we get to be that holy, we are too holy.

There was always in the heart of the Galilean a spot reserved for forgiveness and compassion. A wise person once said upon seeing another in a very bad condition, "There, except by the grace of God, am I."

We are taught to pray: "Forgive us our sins as we forgive those who sinned against us." In other words, our forgiveness depends on our forgiving. If you can't forgive, don't expect any forgiveness.

It takes no special talent to forgive. You don't have to have the mind of a genius. Only a loving and compassionate heart. And that comes from attitude and practice, not from great knowledge.

"Let the person among you who is without sin throw the first stone." It is good to remember that when we are ready to condemn another. For it is so easy to do, this casting of stones, and often so tempting.

I think I'm going to get a rock and put it on my desk. On it I will write The First Stone. Then when I'm inclined to throw verbal stones at another who has done wrong I will look at that stone and recall the story of Jesus and the woman caught in adultery. I will remember the forgiveness and compassion he had for someone who had done wrong and was sorry.

One stone is all I need. For there is no danger that I will ever use it. You see, I don't qualify.

The Unobtrusiveness of God

One of the great surprises about God which I have learned to look for is his unobtrusiveness. We make all our plans concerning the coming of God—how God is supposed to act in history, what he is supposed to do—then when we have it all figured out how he is supposed to come and act, we find him doing exactly the opposite.

God did this at Bethlehem. Certainly no one expected God to break into history in such a manner as that. A carpenter father, a peasant mother, and a manger for a crib! Everyone knew that God would come in a manner worthy of God, and the whole world would bow down to him. But he didn't, and they didn't!

God did this again in Joseph's carpentry shop in Nazareth. One who had such an important task as Jesus should surely receive better training than that afforded him at the local synagogue and more advantages than those of a common carpenter. And because he was only the son of a local carpenter, the people in the synagogue drove him out of town. They knew that no carpenter's son could be the Messiah.

If only God would act like God, then we common folk wouldn't have such a hard time recognizing him. We look for God in the great and powerful, but he comes in the small and humble.

I worshiped once in the St. George Anglican Church in Jerusalem. It was a high church, very formal worship service. The music was beyond reach of the common person. The minister spoke above my level of comprehension. In general it was a situation devoid of the things we generally associate with a warm service. But as I sat in that pew a group of children passed by on the way to their seat. It was a group of half-blind children leading those who were totally blind to a seat where they could worship God. And I want to tell you that I felt the greatness and grandeur of God when those children walked by.

We look for God in the great and mighty, and he comes in the love of poor blind children. Truly the prophet was right when he wrote, "Your ways are not my ways, neither are your thoughts my thoughts."

What is it about God which captivates us? It is that he who was able to call legions of armies to his aid chose instead to enter Jerusalem as a penniless prophet riding on the back of a donkey. He did not come on a great white stallion with sword in hand and fist doubled, ready to strike the first one who stepped in his path. But he came as a preacher of peace with no uniform but the seamless robe of a peasant and no power over men except the power given him in each individual heart.

This is one of the great surprises of God—his unobtrusiveness. Look for him, if you wish, in the big and the high and the mighty and the great. But if you wish to find him, then you must search for him in the least and the last and the lost.

Decisions

Who knows how much is at stake in the decisions we make every day? We decide to do something which seems so small, and it ends up shaping our whole life.

I chose one day to become a Christian. I never realized when I made that choice how far reaching the effects would be. It didn't seem to be such an earth-shaking choice at the time. I just looked at the options available as to a way of life, and the Christian faith made more practical sense than any of the others.

I am old enough now to know that that decision was the wisest choice I have ever made. Because of my Christian faith I have been able to fit together the pieces of life's puzzle.

I was in a big city recently and while there I watched the people who walked the streets. There were three young people who were cursing loud and clear, threatening to kill another person they knew if such and such a thing happened.

I walked past the bars and they were crowded. The music was loud and the booze was flowing. Supposedly, the people were there to have a good time. But that sure looked like a miserable way to have a good time.

I spoke to a few people I met on the street. A few

spoke back. Most ignored me. Some looked at me as if I was rather stupid for offering a smile.

Every person is what he is because of the decisions he has made. Of course each of us is influenced tremendously by others in the decisions we make. But, in the final analysis, we do our own deciding.

As I said before, we hardly ever realize the range of effects that our decisions will have on our life. We choose this or that, we go one way or another, and when we do it brings us a certain kind of life.

It is wise, as we travel along this road of life, for each of us to have a destination picked out where we wish to arrive. Then, each immediate decision which we are called upon to make can be made in light of the destination for which we are traveling. Unless we do this, our immediate decisions can be totally unrelated, and we will not have any idea where we will end up until we are already there.

Each of us will have to go on making decisions, for this process is a part of life. And after we make our decisions, our decisions then make us.

Like I said, one never knows how far reaching the effects of a decision will be. I made a decision one day to follow the Way. It has affected my life more than any other decision I have ever made. And the longer I live the happier I am that I made the decision I did.

The Bargain Watch

Once, outside Rome on our way to Naples, we stopped at a restaurant for a rest stop. When we were returning to our bus, we met a couple of men who were peddling watches. They were trying to sell to several members of our group. I noticed a couple who were looking at one watch.

The man was asking one hundred thirty dollars for the watch. They looked at it for a moment and then gave it back to the man. He then approached me and asked if I wanted it. I told him no, I wasn't interested. He then pulled me aside and said he would let me have it for eighty dollars. Though I wasn't interested in the watch, my bargaining curiosity was aroused, and I told him that it was still too high. He wanted to know if I was the tour leader. I told him that I was. That being the case, he said, he would let me have it for fifty dollars.

I looked at the watch again. It was an Omega. Although my knowledge of watches was limited, I remembered that Omega was a pretty good brand of watch. I looked at it a little closer. It looked like a good buy, but the fact remained that I didn't need the watch. I had a good one.

I thought about it for a minute and then shook my head and told him I wasn't interested. But he was persistent, and as I walked toward the bus he asked what I would give for it. Being kinda ridiculous, I told him I would give ten dollars. He balked a little and tried to act insulted.

I walked on to the bus. He approached some others and tried to sell the watch to them. None was interested. Finally, just before we were ready to leave, he came to the bus and told me he would take twenty dollars. I kinda laughed a little, reached into my pocket, and pulled out a ten-dollar bill. Again he acted insulted. But as the door was being closed, he ran up, grabbed my ten dollars, and handed me the watch. All the way home I thought about my bargain. A watch which he had asked one hundred thirty dollars for I had bought for only ten dollars! It isn't every day you have a chance at a bargain like that.

After I had been home a few days the watch stopped running. I carried it to the repair shop to get it fixed. It was there that I learned that the watch I had bought was not an Omega at all, but an imitation—counterfeit. I had been taken. My bargain was no bargain at all.

Many times I have thought about that incident and remembered the lesson it taught me. There are many areas to which this truth applies. For instance, many people are attracted to the Christian faith when the cross is left out. Like I was with the watch, they are looking for a bargain. But before long they become disillusioned. Then they have to face the truth. Christianity minus the cross is no bargain at all—it is counterfeit. Remember that the next time you are offered Christianity at a bargain.

Politics—The Christian's Responsibility

Politics—the Christian's responsibility. It is a subject that is certainly relevant, but one that has been ignored long and often. Because, you see, the Christian does have some political responsibility.

To begin with, the Christian has a responsibility not to accept the common belief that politics is a crooked business without doing something to correct it. Too long we have accepted politics as being inherently evil. For years I have been informed that politics is a crooked business, and that it's crookedness was to be accepted.

Politics does not have to be crooked. It is not crooked even by nature. Whatever is crooked about politics is so partly because we have allowed it. As Christians we have a responsibility to make government as honest and fair and efficient as it can be.

Not only that, but the Christian has a responsibility of recognizing elected officials as humans capable of making mistakes. No person is infallible. And simply because an official makes a mistake, or even more than one mistake, doesn't automatically make him a "crooked politician." And remember that no person, or group of persons, can solve everybody's problems.

Still another responsibility of the Christian is to be involved in the political process. "All that is necessary for the triumph of evil," wrote Edmund Burke, "is that good men do nothing." In many elections, if not in most elections, less than 50 percent of the qualified voters even bother to vote.

Too often we have divorced Christian commitment from social, political responsibility. Separation of church and state does not mean separation of Christian faith and civic responsibility. "God so loved the world." Not just the church, but the world!

As Christians, it is our responsibility not to be concerned with "What's best for me," but "What is best for our city, state, or nation." We have an obligation to support principles rather than prejudices.

Many times we have criticized without contributing. I'm reminded of the man I visited once who told me everything that was wrong with the church. The only problem was that he had not been inside a church building in twenty years! Sometimes we are that way with politics. In the past two years, how many of us have contributed one dollar or one hour to a good cause or candidate? How many of us even bothered to vote in the last election?

The church has been terribly slow to recognize the responsibility of individual Christians to be involved in the political process. If anything, the emphasis has been for the Christian to stay clear of the "crooked world of politics."

The Christian has a responsibility to use his Christian commitment for social good. How? Well, for one thing, by encouraging and supporting good candidates. In order to have better officials we must have better candidates.

I remember hearing a lecturer say once that a person's private moral life did not affect his ability to serve a public office. As I listened, I wanted to tell him that he was stupid, but I knew I could never convince him of the fact. However, we are beginning to see now, quite clearly, that personal moral standards do affect a person's ability to serve in public office.

As Christians, we do have responsibilities in the area of politics. How well we fulfill those responsibilities will determine the type of government we will have—from the local precinct to the national level.

Good Things Still Happen

It was Thanksgiving Day. John P. Walter was lying in a hospital bed in Lubbock, Texas. Walter had to visit the hospital often. In order to keep living, he takes kidney treatments three times a week.

Making the trips to the hospital had sent Walter's hospital bills zooming. But worse than that, his health had meant that he was unable to harvest his cotton crop, and it was in danger of rotting.

While millions of Americans were taking the day off to enjoy the traditional Thanksgiving turkey, some of Walter's neighbors and friends were spending the day in a different way.

"We knew he needed help, but would never ask for it," said a friend of Walter's. "He understands we all have crops we need to get out of the field at this time. But he needed help, so we all came." His friends came all right. On that Thanksgiving Day more than twenty cotton harvesters were in operation on Walter's two hundred acres of cotton.

"We just decided to heck with it," said H. G. Burkett, Jr., who with Allen Hagens spearheaded the community effort. "We decided to help him first and then worry about ourselves."

Why, a local grocery store even supplied food for those working, and some of the wives prepared it. And at the College Avenue Co-op Gin everyone else's processing had to stop so that there would be adequate trailers to carry Walter's cotton.

Distillate fuel had been in short supply in the west Texas area for several weeks, but the men who brought their machinery decided to use their own fuel for the special harvest. About that, Hagens had this to say, "If we used Johnny's fuel, he would not have any for future needs."

Walter was prevented from attending the Thanksgiving harvest because of his six-hour appointment for the kidney treatment. "I've always been blessed with good neighbors," he said. "This is one Thanksgiving I'll never forget."

Pick up your local daily newspaper, or turn on your radio or television, and chances are too much of the news will be bad news—killings, robbings, rapes, and the like. Being continually bombarded with bad news has a harmful effect on us. We begin to think that the only things which happen are bad.

Never believe that! Good things still happen. Lots of good things happen. All across this country of ours there are people helping other people. You may never read about them or hear about them, but good things are still happening. In big cities and in little towns all across the land, good things are happening because good people are making them happen.

One wonders who received the most—Walter or his friends. One thing is for certain, they all benefited from the sharing.

Yes, sir, the spirit of Christ still dwells in the hearts of some men. If you doubt it, ask Johnny Walter about it. He can give you a first-hand report.

A Matter of Priorities

In the normal pursuit of life, the average person of seventy has spent three years in education, eight years in amusement, six years in eating, eleven years in working, twenty-four years in sleeping, five and a half years in washing and dressing, six years in walking, three years in conversation, three years in reading, and one-half year in worshiping God.

We are all equal when it comes to the amount of time we have. We may be different in every other aspect of life, but in time we are all equal. Each of us has twenty-four hours every day. No more. No less. What we do with our time is determined by what we consider important. We have time for our business because we consider it important. We have time for recreation because it is important. We have time for the family because the family is important. The things we consider most important we always have time for. The things we consider less important we leave for a more "convenient" time.

The person who doesn't have time for God has identically the same amount of time as the person who always has time for God. It is simply a matter of priorities—the things we consider most important. Never use a busy schedule as an excuse for ignorance in spiritual matters. If we consider God important enough, we will find time for him.

The person who doesn't have time for the church doesn't consider the church very important, regardless of what he says. One person can drive for hours to get to a ball game, make plans for weeks in advance to be certain he has the time to go. But that same person can't block out a single hour to worship God or drive three minutes to participate in the church worship service. It is simply a matter of what we consider more important.

I knew a person who spent twelve to fifteen hours each week keeping his yard in immaculate condition. But he never took sixty minutes to check the condition of his soul. A beautiful yard was more important than a beautiful soul. It was simply a matter of priorities.

One thing the Galilean does is to help us keep our priorities in proper perspective. He solved this matter of priorities one day on a mountainside above the Sea of Galilee. He said, "Seek first the kingdom of God." That one statement solves the problem of what is most important in life.

What life needs is a proper balance, always making sure that the most important things are in the most important places.

Two Kinds of Sin

Some time ago I had a tooth with a bad cavity. The edge of the tooth was so sharp that it cut my tongue. I called the dentist to get an appointment and was told that it would be a couple of weeks before the dentist could fill the tooth, but if I would come down to the office he would smooth the tooth off so that it would not cut my tongue.

I went down to his office. He fixed the tooth so that it would not hurt, and then he took some X-rays of my teeth. I was told to come back in two weeks.

Well, two weeks later I went back to the dentist. I was happy that the cavity was to be filled. It certainly needed filling. It was one of the largest cavities I had ever had. But when I sat down in the chair, the dentist informed me that he was not going to fill that cavity. I asked him why not. He told me that the X-rays had revealed a larger, more serious cavity in an upper jaw tooth on the other side. It was far more important, he explained, that he correct the hidden cavity. So, for the next hour, work was spent correcting a cavity which I didn't even know existed.

After I left the dentist's office, I began thinking about how much like sin those two cavities were. I compared them with the two types of sin—the sins of the flesh and the sins of the spirit.

Too often, our emphasis has been on the sins of

the flesh—drinking, cursing, running around. I'm afraid that many times we have considered the sins of the flesh as the only sins, certainly as the major ones.

We have ignored the sins of the spirit, sins like stinginess and prejudice and a bad attitude. The problem with sins of the spirit is that they are not surface sins, they are deeper, hidden sins. The sins of the spirit are far more dangerous and far more difficult to detect and get at than sins of the flesh. Indeed, like the hidden cavity, it often takes a very close examination to even know they exist. But they are certainly just as deadly as the sins of the flesh.

Well, the dentist eventually filled my cavities— the one I knew about and the one I didn't. The thing that scares me so is that the one I didn't know existed was far more serious than the one that bothered me.

I'll tell you what my trip to the dentist has made me do in my spiritual life. It has made me examine myself more closely in order to discover and correct the sins of the spirit. For I am convinced that quite often they are more deadly than the sins of the flesh. And I don't want to have a decayed soul because of them.

About Public Worship

In 1782 James Price, a British scientist, announced that he had discovered a method of changing base metals into silver and gold. He was honored by King George III and his feat was acclaimed by many. But when members of the royal society asked him to repeat his experiment, his response was committing suicide by drinking poison!

Now, what has that got to do with us? Many people are like that when it comes to public worship. They boast about their ability to worship the Creator at home or traveling or fishing or golfing or in any number of other places. They don't need to attend public worship. But when it comes time to back up their boasting with facts, they often find that they commit suicide of their souls.

I can think of three good, solid reasons why we should attend public worship regularly. First of all, there is the need for fellowship. Man cannot live alone. He needs fellowship with others. John Donne once wrote, "No man is an island, entire of itself; every man is a piece of the continent, a part of the main." This is true of worship as well as other areas of life. James W. Clarke stated in a newsletter for Presbyterian men, "Man is a religious animal, and if he holds aloof from public worship he starves and stunts his highest instincts. If a man is to come to his full stature, he must come to it inside the church."

Of course, he meant the fellowship of the church and not the building.

The second need for public worship is that of scholarship. Rare, indeed, is the person who grows in his knowledge and understanding of our Maker apart from the church. I have met several people who have stated that they had no need for the church, that they could "make it by myself." I don't know what they were making of themselves, but it was not persons true to the Creator's desire. They usually ended up making self-serving individuals.

The other reason that I feel the need for public worship is exactly that—worship. Man will instinctively worship something. How he directs his instincts will determine what he worships. Without the guidance and direction which comes from public worship, he usually satisfies his hunger with some substitute for the real God.

Of course, one reason so many stay away from public worship is that it is a threat to them. They may have to change, and change comes slowly and reluctantly for many. It is a dangerous thing to attend public worship for those who are satisfied with themselves. There is always the chance God will break through their protective shield and soften their resistive spirit.

These, then, are the reasons I believe in public worship. I call them the three ships—fellowship, scholarship, and worship.

I know I can't make silver and gold from base metals, and I certainly don't want to commit suicide of my soul. It is the most lasting part of me I have.

The Story of Old Joe

Let me tell you the story of Old Joe.

Old Joe was one of those fellows who didn't like to be pushed around. He was just tired of paying taxes, didn't like the way the government was being run, and in general had had it with anything that smacked of authority. In fact, Old Joe didn't even like to pull over for emergency vehicles. He felt that they just used their sirens to get through traffic about 99 percent of the time.

Old Joe was driving through some heavy traffic one day when an ambulance pulled up behind him. It's siren was wailing loud and clear. Old Joe looked in his mirror and saw the ambulance coming up his lane. Since there was heavy traffic, Old Joe knew that the ambulance couldn't get through unless he pulled over. Very shortly the ambulance was on Old Joe's bumper. Inside himself he was wondering if he should pull over to let the vehicle pass.

Then a brilliant idea flashed in Old Joe's mind. Now was the time to get even with those people who drive ambulances! Old Joe made the decision that he would stay in his lane and keep that ambulance from passing. He laughed inside himself because the opportunity had presented itself.

The ambulance kept its siren going at full blast. But Old Joe, determined to get even, just kept driving his leisurely slow pace. In fact, he even slowed down a little. The ambulance driver began to blow his horn and motion for Old Joe to move over. But Old Joe did exactly as he wanted to do. He didn't move over and he didn't pay any attention to the ambulance driver. He simply acted as if he didn't hear the siren.

For quite a distance Old Joe kept that ambulance from passing. He managed to get his car in position several times at key locations to make sure that the ambulance couldn't pass.

Following several minutes of keeping the ambulance behind him, Old Joe soon approached the street which led to his house. He was tempted not to turn, just to keep the emergency vehicle behind him for a longer time. But when he got to the street that led to his house he decided that he had had enough fun and turned. While making his turn he was thinking that he had showed them, he had gotten even and wasn't going to be pushed around any more.

But when he turned, the ambulance turned also. This pleased Old Joe tremendously, because he could still keep it from passing for a few more houses.

When he got to his house, Old Joe gave his signal and turned into his driveway. But, much to his surprise, the ambulance turned into his driveway also. He had seen the anger on the ambulance driver's face, and Old Joe figured that the driver had followed him to fight. So Old Joe jumped out of his car, ran to the ambulance, jerked open the driver's door, and started fighting. By the time the other attendant and some of the neighbors could get things under control, Old Joe's wife was at the door shouting, "Where have you been with that ambulance? You should have been here ten minutes ago! Little Joe is barely breathing!"

Well, they finally got Little Joe to the hospital. The doctor said if they had been there ten minutes earlier he might have lived. Old Joe, he got even all right. But in getting even, he lost. Life usually works that way.

Is this a true story? The incident could be. The moral it teaches is.

On Being Afraid

Flying is a frightening experience for some people. For others it is a thoroughly enjoyable experience. The reason flying is frightening for most people is that they haven't done much of it, don't know a lot about it. We humans have a natural tendency to fear that which is unknown to us.

I can remember an incident that happened to me once as we were leaving Paris. The plane was climbing to its cruising altitude shortly after take-off. Then, suddenly, the captain cut back on the power. I knew that the two most crucial times in flying were taking off and landing. The clouds were thick, and I could hardly see the end of the plane's wing. I had not flown very much and I became very scared. I was afraid something was wrong. However, after a few minutes the captain increased the power again and climbed to the cruising altitude.

A few years later a similar incident occurred as we were leaving Atlanta on our way to New York. As we were climbing, the captain suddenly cut back on the power. We were about eight or nine thousand feet high. He held this altitude for about five minutes. Then the plane began a slow banking turn. I leaned over to tell my brother who was sitting next to me that something was wrong.

In a few moments the captain announced that we had a wing flap which was not working properly and that we were going back to Atlanta. We circled the airport for a few minutes, time to allow emergency vehicles on the ground to get into position. When we landed we saw the fire engines and ambulances parked along the runway, lights flashing. The landing was near perfect, and in a few minutes a crew was working on our craft.

But you know, during that emergency landing I wasn't frightened at all. Had it happened during my first few flights I would have probably died of a heart attack!

What was the difference? Well, I had become accustomed to flying. I knew more about it and realized that the craft was under the control of an experienced pilot. My experience and knowledge had taught me that I really didn't have any reason to be afraid.

Aristotle, the wise Greek philosopher, once said, "Fear is pain arising from the anticipation of evil." Well, I didn't expect anything evil or bad to happen when that plane landed. I expected exactly what I got—a safe landing.

It was Emerson who wrote, "Fear always springs from ignorance." You know, I believe he was right about that. That we fear what we don't understand. There are multitudes of people who fear God. They fear him because they don't know him. If they would only make an attempt to know him they would soon quit fearing him and begin to love him.

Well, my fear of flying is gone. In fact, flying has

become a thoroughly enjoyable experience for me. The reason for this change is that I have become more knowledgeable about it.

And no person has to fear God, either. The more you know about him, the more you love him and realize how great his love is for you. And the more you love him the more you enjoy him.

It is a good thing for a man to turn his fear of God into love of God.

Perseverance

Someone once asked a wise old minister for his definition of perseverance. His definition was a simple, yet profound one. "It means, first of all, to take hold; second, to hold on; third and last, to never let go."

I began thinking about his definition and decided it was worth looking into.

Perseverance. It means first of all to take hold. Where does one start in life? Where does he begin? He begins by taking hold, finding something which gives meaning to life. Life doesn't really begin for a person until he finds meaning in it.

Henry David Thoreau was a philosopher who searched for some meaning in life. In his search he found something which gave it purpose, meaning. The story is told about Thoreau being in jail. He lived in a state where a poll tax was charged before a person was allowed to vote. Because of his stand against that tax he ended up in jail. While he was in jail his good friend Ralph Waldo Emerson came to visit him. Emerson looked at his friend behind the bars and spoke, "Why, Henry, what are you doing in there?" Thoreau was quick with his reply. "Nay, Ralph, the question is not what am I doing in here. The question is what are you doing out there?"

Thoreau had found meaning in life. He had found something to take hold of. His reply was his way of letting his friend know that.

Take hold. Find meaning in life. That's what the Christian faith is all about. "I have come that you may have life, abundant life." You don't have an abundant life unless there is meaning to life.

Of course there are those who turn their backs on this search for meaning. They refuse to try to find any meaning, saying life can have no meaning, that it is meaningless. Well, if you are going to persevere in life, you must find first of all something to take hold of.

Then, the wise old minister said, perseverance means to hold on. Do you ever get tired, tired of doing the same old thing day after day and feel that you never see any results from your labors?

Maybe you have heard about the two men who were pushing a rather large object. They would push and grunt, and push and grunt, and push and grunt. Getting tired they decided to take a rest. While resting, one of them came up with what he considered a brilliant plan. He turned to his partner and spoke. "Listen. I've got an idea how we can make this job a lot easier for the two of us. There's no need for both of us to push and grunt." "What's your idea?" asked the other. "Well, let's make things easier by dividing our responsibilities. You push and I'll grunt." I hesitate to tell you that his plan was not enthusiastically received by his partner.

Well, there are those who get tired of pushing and grunting, who decide to let another do the pushing while they do the grunting. And their approach only makes things tougher for all of us.

You would be surprised at the number of people who have grown tired, tired of trying, and have given up. You can see this tiredness in family life—with the responsibility of raising children. A great number of parents have quit trying to help their children in the struggle to become mature, responsible adults. The struggle is too long and too hard. So they turn their children loose to do as they please. Who suffers the most when the parents quit? Why, the children, of course.

I'm reminded of the little girl who planted an oak seed one day and then became very angry the next day when she went to check on it and discovered that it had not grown into a mighty oak tree. My nephew came home from his first day at school disgusted. "Why?" his mother asked. "Because they didn't teach me to read!" he replied.

Well, you can't grow an oak tree in a day nor teach a child to read in an hour. Neither can you raise a child in a week. In the Old Testament there is the story of the Israelites leaving their slavery in Egypt and heading for the Promised Land. The trip which shouldn't have taken them more than forty days actually took them forty years. En route they became disgruntled and often wanted to return to Egypt and slavery. The roads to our promised lands are often longer than we think or like or are willing to accept.

In First Samuel there is the story of a messenger who reported to Eli on the progress of a battle. His first words were, "I fled the battle today." That's what many are doing even to this day—fleeing the battle, giving up, quitting. It takes courage for a person to hold on when nothing is going right. "I fled the battle today. It looked like we were losing. So I quit. I ran."

It takes no special courage to flee, to quit, to run, to give up—on anything. But to stay and fight, that's another matter.

Remember the incident in the Gospels when many decided to flee from Christ. They were following him because they wanted to get something from him. But when it became apparent that they would be required to give something, they ran! Christ turned to his close disciples and asked the question, "Will you also turn away?" It was Peter who answered him. "Lord, to whom shall we go? You have the words of eternal life." Because of Christ, Peter had found meaning in life.

A person can stay with something as long as it has meaning. Sometimes we get tired. Tired even in our Christian faith. We think of leaving it. Giving it up. What do you propose we replace it with? Certainly if we are going to replace it the replacement should be something better, an improvement over what we have. No man voluntarily leaves one job to take another unless he considers it an improvement. Surely we should do no less with our faith. How can you improve yourself when you already have hold of the best life has to offer?

God doesn't need more people who will stay with him when everything is going smoothly. That kind of follower is a dime a dozen. But he is in search of those who will keep on keeping on when it appears they aren't making any progress. It is our responsibility to be faithful—not necessarily successful. We are to be faithful and leave the results of our labors to God.

Perseverance means, second, to hold on.

Third, the wise old minister said, perseverance means to never let go. That's a thought to wrap your minds around—never let go. God isn't after a miracle-worker who can change the world overnight. The reason is that no such person exists. But he does want someone who will stay with him regardless of what happens. Someone who will never let go.

God has put his only requirement for the Christian life—faithfulness—within reach of each of us. Henry Willard Austin reminded us of this thought when he wrote:

> Genius, that power which dazzles mortal eyes,
> Is oft but perseverance in disguise.

One thing which causes us to grow tired in our Christian faith is our feeling of incompetence, our feeling that we aren't equipped for the battle. And, oddly enough, this should be one of the lesser of our concerns. God makes available to us instruments with which to face the battle. It is up to us to use them.

While a seminary student, my speech teacher shared this piece of literature by Edward Rowland Sill with me:

This I beheld, or dreamed it in a dream:
There spread a cloud of dust along a plain;
And underneath the cloud, or in it, raged
A furious battle, and men yelled, and swords
Shocked upon swords and sheilds. A prince's banner
Wavered, then staggered backward, hemmed by foes.
A craven hung along the battle's edge
And thought, "Had I a sword of keener steel—
That blue blade that the king's son bears—
but this
Blunt thing—!" He snapt and flung it from his hand,
And, lowering, crept away and left the field.
Then came the king's son, wounded, sore bestead,
And weaponless, and saw the broken sword,
Hilt-buried in the dry and trodden sand,
And ran and snatched it, and with battle-shout
Lifted afresh, he hewed his enemy down,
And saved a great cause that heroic day.

The difference between the real Christian and the play Christian is that when the battle appears lost, the play Christian will flee the battle, but the real Christian will take whatever instrument God provides and use it in the battle.

Paul got tired of it all once. But after thinking more deeply about it he had this to say, "For I am convinced that nothing can ever separate us from his love. Death can't, and life can't. The angels won't, and all the powers of hell itself cannot keep God's love away. Our fears for today, our worries about tomorrow, or where we are—high above the sky, or in the deepest ocean—nothing will ever be able to separate us from the love of God demonstrated by our Lord Jesus Christ when he died for us." Basically, Paul was saying, "I will stay with the Christian faith."

Never give up on your faith. Never let go. Life has little meaning when you lose your faith. Why should one make an effort to raise a child when he has lost faith in the child? Why should one be concerned about the church when he has lost faith in it? Why should one care about God when he has lost faith in God, or about himself when he doesn't believe in himself?

In Galatians, Paul writes, "Never get tired of doing good." The wise old minister said, "Never let go." Just remember you aren't alone in this struggle. "The Lord shall lead his people as they fight . . . . The Lord God shall sound the trumpet call and go out against his enemies like a whirlwind off the desert from the south." The trumpet of God shall sound. Listen for the trumpet.

He has sounded forth the trumpet that shall never call
   retreat,
He is shifting out the hearts of men before his judgment
   seat.
Oh, be swift, my soul, to answer Him! Be jubilant, my feet!
   Our God is marching on.

"Perseverance means, first of all, to take hold; second, to hold on; third and last, to never let go."